Wipe-Clean

# Trucks and Diggers Activities

Illustrated by Gareth Williams
Designed by Laura Hammonds
Written by Kirsteen Robson

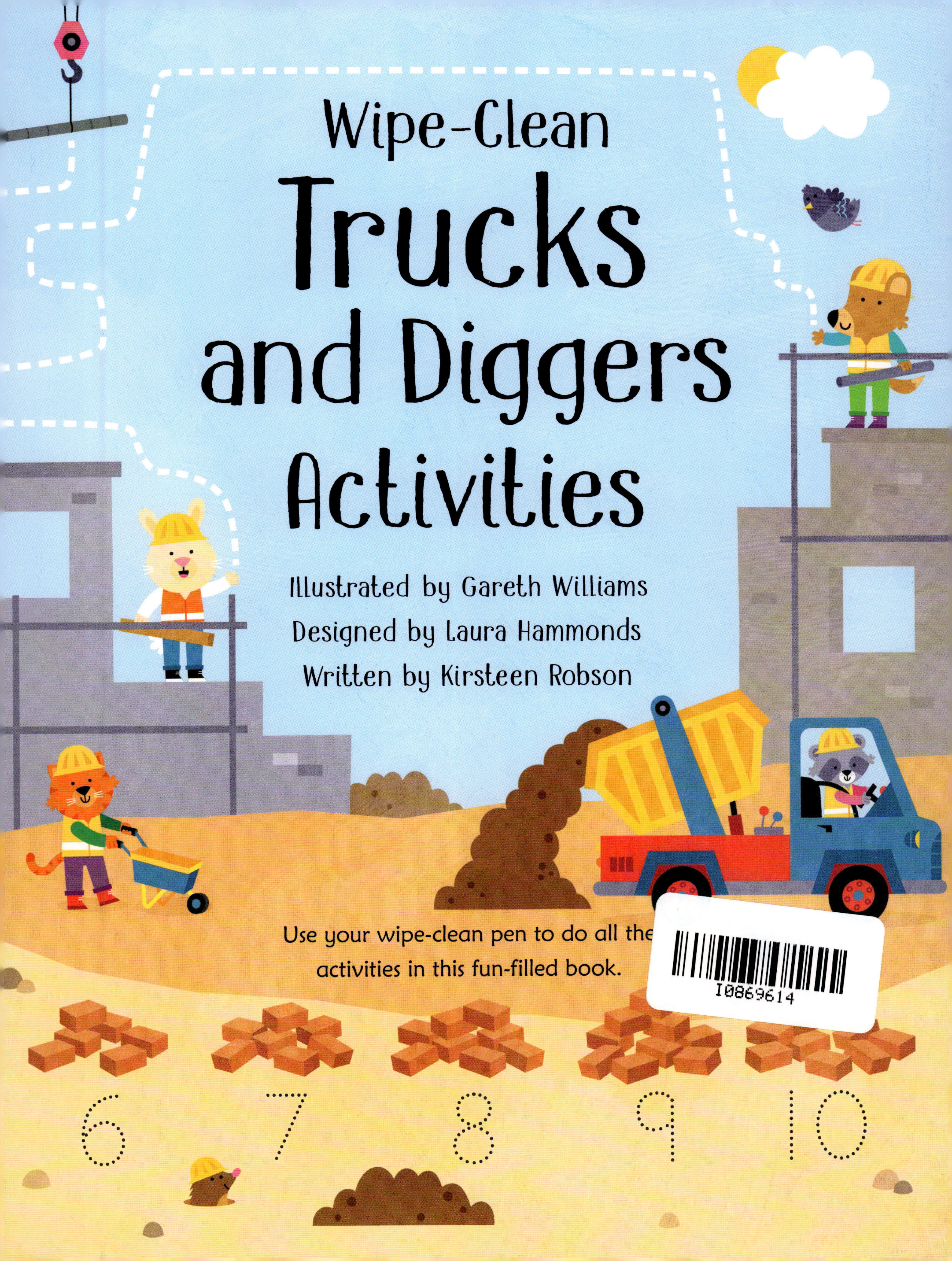


Use your wipe-clean pen to do all the activities in this fun-filled book.

# In the street

Connect the numbered dots in order, to finish the car on the tow truck.

Spot 3 differences between these two recycling collectors.

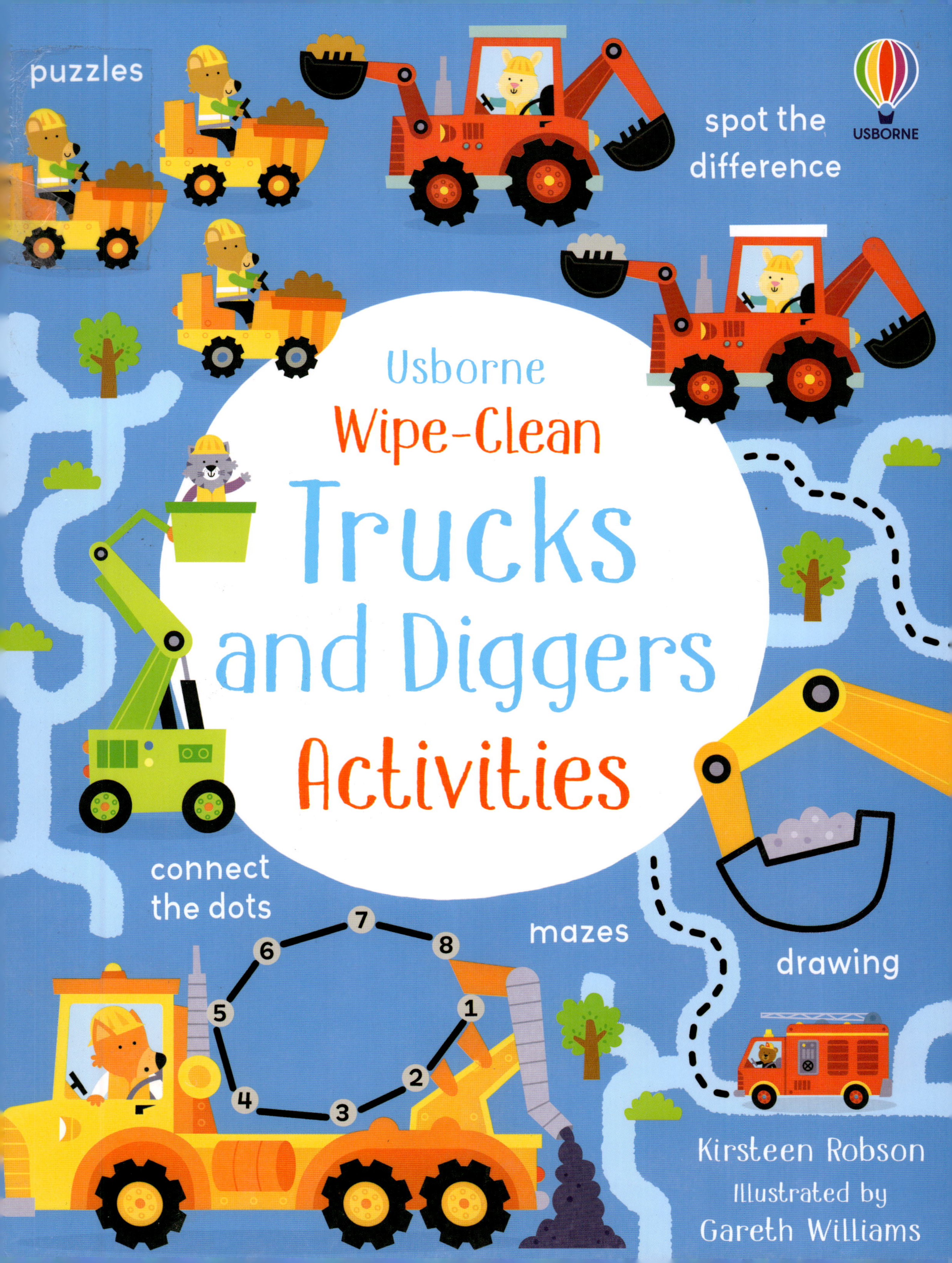


Usborne

# Wipe-Clean Trucks and Diggers Activities

Kirsteen Robson
Illustrated by
Gareth Williams

Follow the trails to see where each metal bar will end up.

Connect the numbered dots in order, to finish the tracked excavator.

Count the piles of bricks, then trace over the numbers.

Count the boxes in each stack below, then trace over the numbers.

Draw over the dotted lines to finish the street sweeper.

Find and circle 6 pigeons.

# On the road

Spot 5 differences between the two delivery trucks above.

Draw over the dotted lines to finish the wheels on the oil tanker.

Count the cars on the car transporter, then trace over the correct number.

4 5 6

Connect the numbered dots in order, to finish the flatbed truck.

# Around the town

Use the pen to show Ivor the way to the park.

Find and circle a bus full of passengers.

Draw over the dotted lines to finish the fire truck.

Draw a line between each matching pair below.

# Construction site

Spot 5 differences between the two cement mixer trucks below.

Draw over the dotted lines to finish the tracked excavators.

Draw over the dotted lines to finish the crane truck.

Follow the trails to see who will take their bricks to Brendan's wall.

# On the farm

Connect the numbered dots in order, to finish the combine harvester.

Write an X under the quadbike and rider below that does not match the others.

Find and circle 3 wheelbarrows.

Draw over the dotted lines to finish the tractor.

Follow the trails to see who will take their apples to Patti.

# Monster trucks

Use the pen to lead The Dragon around the course to the finish.

Draw over the dotted lines to finish the red and blue monster trucks.

Draw around the animal below that is not one of a matching pair.

Draw more wheel tracks, like these.

# At the airport

Draw over the dotted lines to finish the food truck.

Connect the sets of numbered dots in order, to finish the stair truck.

Draw a long line to finish the fuel hose between Bayu and Franz.

Find and circle 10 traffic cones.

Spot 5 differences between these two baggage trucks.

# In the warehouse

Brady

Use the pen to show Brady the way to drive her forklift to Carter in the delivery truck.

Write an X under the picture below that does not match the others.

Find and circle 6 mice.

Draw over the dotted lines to finish the cherry picker.

# Demolition site

Spot 6 differences between the two yellow backhoe loaders.

Connect the sets of numbered dots in order, to finish the excavator.

Draw over the dotted line to finish the wrecking ball.

Follow the trail below and count the small piles of rubble this bulldozer will scoop up. Then trace over the correct number.

# Digging up the road

Draw over the dotted lines to finish the road roller.

Follow the trails to see who will help Doug and Kat lay the pipes.

Write an X under the car below that does not match the others.

Draw lines to show which long pipe needs to go in each hole.

Draw over the dotted lines to finish the water spouting from the broken pipe.

Usborne

Wipe-Clean

# Trucks and Diggers

## Activities

This fun book is a perfect way for young children to develop their counting, observation and pen control skills.

US $8.99
CAN $11.99

JFMAMJ ASOND/25 9549/3

Ink from pen may not be washable.
L'encre du feutre ne s'efface pas toujours au lavage.
This product conforms to ASTM D 4236.

WARNING! Not suitable for children under 36 months because of small parts. Choking hazard.

ATTENTION! Ne convient pas aux enfants de moins de 36 mois en raison des petites pièces. Risque de suffocation par ingestion.

**WARNING:**
**CHOKING HAZARD—Small parts.**
**Not for children under 3 yrs.**

FSC
www.fsc.org
MIX
Paper | Supporting responsible forestry
FSC® C017606

ISBN 978-1-83605-222-7
50899
9 781836 052227

usborne.com

Usborne Publishing Limited, 83-85 Saffron Hill, London EC1N 8RT, United Kingdom. Printed in China.